Shirley's Shops

Allan Ahlberg

Colin McNaughton

WALKER BOOKS

LONDON

In Shirley's sweet shop
there are:

6 lollipops

5 chocolate buttons

4 toffees

3 jelly babies

2 Smarties

1 bubble-gum

…and no customers!

In Shirley's dog shop
there are:

a big dog

a little dog

a very little dog

a round dog

 a square dog

two spotty dogs...

I'm off!

...and a hot dog!

In Shirley's honey shop there are pots of honey...

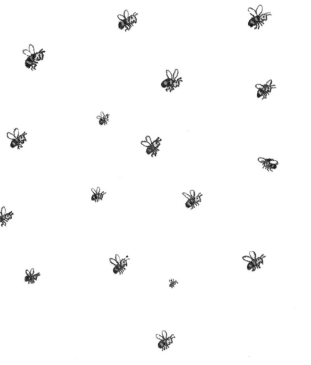

...and lots of bees!

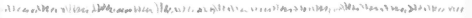

In Shirley's ghost shop there is 1 ghost

and nothing else –
not even Shirley!

In Shirley's sock shop
there are 13 socks —
but only 2 of them match.

In Shirley's weather shop
there are:

rain

fog

snow

wind

blue skies and sunny periods

In Shirley's invisible shop
there are lots of things –

but you can't see them!

In Shirley's fancy-dress shop there are:

coats

hats

a wolf mask

shoes

a wand

dresses

...and a prize for
the winner!

In Shirley's tea shop
there are:

cups and plates

knives, forks and spoons

cakes and biscuits

crisps and sandwiches

pop…

...and a few friends.

The End

Picture
Dictionary

mum and dad

paint

teddy

doll

bucket

umbrella

cat

jar

sock

shop